Fox Family Adventures

Bobbie Kalman
Crabtree Publishing Company
www.crabtreebooks.com

Animal Family ADVENTURES

Created by Bobbie Kalman

Dedicated by Judy Cooper
To my very special grandson Hayden
With all my love—Nannie

Author
Bobbie Kalman

Photo research
Bobbie Kalman

Editors
Kathy Middleton
Crystal Sikkens

Design
Bobbie Kalman
Katherine Berti

Print and production coordinator
Katherine Berti

Photographs
Animals Animals: © Maier, Robert: page 5 (bottom)
Corel: page 22 (top)
Superstock: Radius: page 17 (top); Brian
   Bevan/ardea.com/Pantheon: page 23 (top)
Thinkstock: pages 5 (top), 27 (coyote), 30, 31
Cover and other images by Shutterstock

Library and Archives Canada Cataloguing in Publication

Kalman, Bobbie, author
          Fox family adventures / Bobbie Kalman.

(Animal family adventures)
Includes index.
Issued in print and electronic formats.
ISBN 978-0-7787-2232-8 (bound).--ISBN 978-0-7787-2240-3
(paperback).--ISBN 978-1-4271-1714-4 (html)

          1. Foxes--Juvenile literature. 2. Foxes--Infancy--Juvenile
literature. I. Title.

QL737.C22K337 2016   j599.775   C2015-908698-1
                                              C2015-908699-X

Library of Congress Cataloging-in-Publication Data

Names: Kalman, Bobbie, author.
Title: Fox family adventures / Bobbie Kalman.
Description: St. Catharines, Ontario ; New York, New York : Crabtree
   Publishing Company, [2016] | Series: Animal family adventures | Includes index.
Identifiers: LCCN 2016008885 (print) | LCCN 2016012797 (ebook) | ISBN
   9780778722328 (reinforced library binding : alk. paper) | ISBN
   9780778722403 (pbk. : alk. paper) | ISBN 9781427117144 (electronic HTML)
Subjects: LCSH: Foxes--Behavior--Juvenile literature. | Foxes--Juvenile
   literature.
Classification: LCC QL737.C22 K3554 2016 (print) | LCC QL737.C22 (ebook) |
   DDC 599.775--dc23
LC record available at http://lccn.loc.gov/2016008885

Crabtree Publishing Company
www.crabtreebooks.com   1-800-387-7650

Printed in Canada/052016/TL20160324

Copyright © **2016 CRABTREE PUBLISHING COMPANY.** All rights reserved. No part of this publication may be reproduced, stored in a retrieval system or be transmitted in any form or by any means, electronic, mechanical, photocopying, recording, or otherwise, without the prior written permission of Crabtree Publishing Company. In Canada: We acknowledge the financial support of the Government of Canada through the Canada Book Fund for our publishing activities.

Published in Canada
Crabtree Publishing
616 Welland Ave.
St. Catharines, Ontario
L2M 5V6

Published in the United States
Crabtree Publishing
PMB 59051
350 Fifth Avenue, 59th Floor
New York, New York 10118

Published in the United Kingdom
Crabtree Publishing
Maritime House
Basin Road North, Hove
BN41 1WR

Published in Australia
Crabtree Publishing
3 Charles Street
Coburg North
VIC 3058

What is in this book?

Meet the fox kits!	4
Body changes	6
Out in the world	8
Fox habitats	10
What will they see?	12
Having fun playing	14
Family members	16
What do they mean?	18
Learning to hunt	20
All kinds of food!	22
Autumn and winter	24
Did you know?	26
Match them up!	28
Draw some foxes!	30
Words to know and Index	32

Meet the fox kits!

Spring is here, and four fox babies, called kits, are born to a red fox mother we shall call Dena. They are born in a **nursery den**, a big hole dug under the ground. Foxes are animals called **mammals**. Mammal mothers make milk in their bodies that they feed to their babies. The kits depend on Dena to feed them milk and keep them warm. She does not leave her babies for the first two weeks. Other foxes in Dena's family bring her food.

After two weeks, Dena leaves the den for a short time each day. Her kits, Sam, Fred, Bonnie, and Kate, are still too small to go out of the den. They snuggle close to one another and wonder where their mother went. They are getting hungry and hope she comes back soon.

Body changes

When they are born, fox kits have brown fur, short noses, small ears, and they are blind and deaf. Their eyes and ears open about two weeks later, and then they can see and hear. Soon, their noses and ears will grow longer, too, just like Dena's. Did you know that foxes have whiskers on their legs as well as on their faces? Whiskers help them find their way in the dark.

Foxes **molt**, or lose their fur, in spring, and grow thinner fur for the summer. Dena is losing much of her fur now. Her kits are still brown, but at five weeks, longer red fur will grow through their short brown fur.

Out in the world

The kits are now a month old. On a warm sunny day, Dena brings them out of the den for the first time. The pups must climb up through a tunnel that leads out of the den and learn to walk on the ground outside. Sam, Bonnie, and Kate have made it out. Fred is behind them. The sun is bright. The kits keep their eyes straight ahead and do not look up.

Sam is a little scared about being out of his den home. He snuggles up to Dena. He feels better knowing she is nearby.

Bonnie, Kate, and Fred have found some weeds. "What can these be?" they wonder. "Are they good to eat?"

9

Fox habitats

Red fox families can live in many kinds of **habitats**, or natural places. They live in areas where they can find plenty of food and water. Some foxes live on mountains or in deserts. Many foxes now make their homes in cities. Dena's family lives in a grassy habitat, called a meadow. It is at the edge of a forest.

Dena has taken Sam to show him where to find water near their den, but Sam prefers to drink Dena's milk instead.

What will they see?

Many kinds of animals live in the forest near the meadow where Dena and her kits live. Which of these animals might the fox kits see? Which ones have you seen?

chipmunk

raccoon

black bear

wood mouse

bobcat kitten

rabbit

Will the kits see some raccoons, chipmunks, or bears climbing trees? Will they see a bobcat kitten or a mother deer licking her baby fawn? What might happen if they meet some skunks? Which animals will the kits hunt when they are older? (See pages 20–21.)

skunks

deer

fawn

13

Having fun playing

Foxes are active mostly at night, but the kits love to play during the day, too. They run, chase one another, and find things to play with. They also love to play-fight. It helps them learn how to hunt other animals. Fred and Sam are wrestling on the grass. Fred is standing over Sam. He wants to show Sam that he is the boss!

Bonnie, Kate, and Sam are having a race. Kate is ahead of the other two. Where is Fred? They look around and see him running behind them. They stop and wait for their brother. Bonnie gives him a hug when he catches up. What a fun time they have had!

Family members

Red fox families are made up of parents and other family members that help look after the kits. Dena **nurses** her kits until they are about six weeks old. At four weeks, they start eating solid food, too, which their family members bring them. At first, the adults **regurgitate**, or bring up food from their stomachs, to feed the kits. As the kits grow bigger, they start eating animals, as well as plants.

The father of the kits is regurgitating food to feed Sam, who was the first to greet him. Later, another fox brings a squirrel for the kits to share. They will need the adult's help to eat this big animal.

What do they mean?

Foxes **communicate**, or exchange information, with one another in different ways. They bark, scream, and let out warning calls to let the others know that there is danger nearby. They also use their faces, ears, tails, body **postures**, and movements to communicate information or feelings. What message is Dena giving Bonnie in the picture below?

Sam and Bonnie are not really fighting. They are play-fighting.

Are Fred and Kate happy or sad? They are holding their tails high, which means they are happy.

Dena sees danger ahead. She covers Kate with her body and barks at a coyote she sees.

Fred is standing over Sam. What is he saying to him? (See page 14.)

19

Learning to hunt

When the kits are five weeks old, Dena and the other family members bring them less food. The kits will soon need to learn how to find their own food. Red foxes hunt other animals, called **prey**. Their prey includes insects, mice, rabbits, squirrels, birds, frogs, fish, lizards, and raccoons. Foxes often **pounce**, or leap, on top of their prey to trap it. Kate is pouncing on a mouse hiding in the grass. Fred is crouching below her. He is afraid that Kate will land on top of him.

Sam is using his senses of sight and smell to hunt a rabbit hiding in the grass. He is **stalking** it by crouching low and being very quiet so the rabbit won't see or hear him. Bonnie has climbed up on a tree trunk to catch a squirrel. With her excellent sight and hearing, she can see and hear her the squirrel moving.

All kinds of food!

Although foxes hunt many kinds of animals, they are **omnivores**. Omnivores are animals that eat plants as well as animals. At the beginning of summer, Dena stopped nursing her kits. Her family is now spreading out over a larger area to look for food. Sam and Fred are looking for insects in a dead log. They will find plenty.

The kits catch fish, hunt birds, and find eggs to eat. Kate is eating the mouse she caught. Fred has found some blackberries to eat. The kits love berries of all kinds, as well as grass, weeds, and mushrooms.

Autumn and winter

Dena's kits are fully grown by autumn and look just like their parents. The kits leave their den area to find more food. In winter, they will also find mates so they can make babies of their own. Dena and the father of her kits stay close to each other and will make more babies. At the end of winter, Dena will look for another den, where her new kits will be born.

At the end of autumn, male foxes compete with one another over females and **territories**. In winter, foxes follow females closely to make babies. By the following spring, new fox kits are born.

Did you know?

You have learned a lot about red foxes in this book, but there are some other facts you may not know. Which of these fox facts are new to you?

Foxes have good senses of hearing and smell. They see well at night. They also have sharp teeth, but they do not chew their food. They rip it into small pieces that they can swallow.

Foxes pick up their kits and carry them by their necks or ears. Being carried like this does not hurt the kits.

fennec fox   red fox   Arctic fox

Foxes lose body heat through their ears. Big ears lose more heat. Small ears help keep heat inside the body. Fennec foxes live in Africa, where it is hot all year. Red foxes live in places with both hot and cold seasons. Arctic foxes live in very cold places. How do the ears of these foxes suit where they live?

Foxes belong to the dog family. They are wild dogs. Wild dogs live in nature. Wolves, coyotes, and jackals are other wild dogs.

coyote   wolf   jackal

Match them up!

The pictures on these pages will help you remember what you have learned about fox families. Match the pictures with the information in the box on the next page.

A

B

C

Match the pictures with the information below.

1. Red fox kits are brown when they are born.
2. The ears and noses of fox kits get longer as they grow.
3. Fox kits are born in a den. After a month, they come outside to run and play.
4. Foxes use their excellent senses of sight, hearing, and smell when they hunt.
5. Baby foxes drink milk from their mother's body.
6. Foxes pounce on their prey to surprise and trap them.

Answers

1. D, 2. C, 3. A, 4. E, 5. B, 6. F

Draw some foxes!

Foxes are beautiful animals that are fun to draw. Use the paintings on this page to help you draw your own fox family.

If you want to be even more creative, try drawing a fox's face like this one. First draw the outline of the head and then add interesting shapes. Fill in each shape using your favorite colors.

Words to know

Note: Some boldfaced words are defined where they appear in the book.

communicate (kuh-MYOO-ni-keyt) verb To exchange feelings and thoughts through speaking, writing, sounds, or gestures

mammal (MAM-uh-l) noun A warm-blooded animal that is covered in hair or fur and gives birth to live young

molt (mohlt) verb To shed and grow new feathers, fur, or skin

nurse (nurs) verb To feed with milk from the body; to be fed mother's milk

nursery den (NUR-suh-ree den) noun A shelter used to have babies

posture (POS-cher) noun The position of the body

pounce (pouns) verb To spring or leap suddenly to catch prey

prey (prey) noun An animal that is hunted and eaten by another animal

regurgitate (ri-GUR-ji-teyt) verb To bring up food or liquid from the stomach

territory (TER-i-tawr-ee) noun An area claimed and defended by an animal or group of animals as their home area

A noun is a person, place, or thing. A verb is an action word that tells you what someone or something does.

Index

bodies 4, 6–7, 18, 26, 27, 29
communication 18–19
den 4, 5, 8, 9, 11, 24, 29
ears 6, 7, 18, 26, 27, 29
fathers (males) 16, 17, 24, 25
food 4, 10, 16, 21, 22–23

forest animals 12–13
fur 6, 7
habitats 10
hunting 13, 14, 20–21, 22, 23, 29
mammals 4
mates 24
molting 7

noses 6, 7, 29
nursing 4, 11, 16, 29
omnivores 22
playing 14–15, 19
prey 20, 29
senses 6, 26, 29
teeth 26
water 10, 11

32